Tracking Your Walk

PUBLISHING

A Ministry of Youth With A Mission
P.O. Box 55787, Seattle, WA 98155

YWAM Publishing is the publishing ministry of Youth With A Mission. Youth With A Mission (YWAM) is an international missionary organization of Christians from many denominations dedicated to presenting Jesus Christ to this generation. To this end, YWAM has focused its efforts in three main areas: 1) Training and equipping believers for their part in fulfilling the Great Commission (Matthew 28:19). 2) Personal evangelism. 3) Mercy ministry (medical and relief work).

For a free catalog of books and materials write or call:
YWAM Publishing
P.O. Box 55787, Seattle, WA 98155
(425) 771-1153 or (800) 922-2143
www.ywampublishing.com

Unless otherwise indicated, Scripture quotations are taken from the Holy Bible, New International Version®, Copyright© 1973, 1978, 1984 by the International Bible Society. Used by permission of Zondervan Publishing House.

Back cover Scripture quotation is taken from the New Revised Standard Version Bible, Copyright© 1989 by the Division of Christian Education on the National Council of the Churches of Christ in the United States of America.

Sources:
1995 Personal Prayer Diary/Daily Planner. YWAM Publishing, PO Box 55787, Seattle, WA 98155
National Geographic Picture Atlas of Our World. National Geographic Society, Washington DC
Webster's College Dictionary. Random House, Inc, 201 E 50th St., New York, NY 10022
Operation World (by Patrick Johnstone). Zondervan Publishing House, 5300 Patterson Ave. SE, Grand Rapids, MI 49530
Concise Dictionary of Religion (by Irving Hexham). InterVarsity Press, PO Box 1400, Downers Grove, IL 60515

Tracking Your Walk
Copyright © 1994 by Jim and Michelle Drake

Published by Youth With A Mission Publishing
P.O. Box 55787
Seattle, WA 98155

Edited and Compiled by Jim and Michelle Drake
Illustrations by Cheryl Knapp

ISBN 0-927545-70-5

Printed in the United States of America.

Acknowledgments

We gratefully acknowledge King's Kids
for contributing their inspiration, research,
critique, and invaluable input.
Special thanks to Marilyn Wishart
for her prayers and many hours of research.
Thanks also to Cindie Logan, the North American
Prayer Task Force Members (Kings Kids),
Dale Kauffman, Lanita Tibbett,
and Donna Briggs for their suggestions and input.
May this journal be a tool to help kids
everywhere reach their world
with the Good News of Jesus Christ.

About the Editors: Jim and Michelle Drake

Jim and Michelle have ministered to youth of all ages since 1983. They served as Youth Pastors and Christian Education Directors in Sioux Falls, SD., pioneering new programs to assist youth in realizing their potential in the kingdom of God. Jim continues to teach and speak at regional youth camps and retreats, focusing primarily on the areas of self-image, relationships, and destiny in the lives of young believers. Both have ministered with Youth With A Mission (YWAM) in the Far East and are currently on staff with YWAM in the Seattle, Washington area.

Why ShOuLd I KeeP a JoURnaL

How good is your memory? Often, events in our lives quickly fade and become foggy, dream-like memories. If we are to face the challenges of our future, we need to remember God's help and faithfulness during hard times in our past. Keeping a journal is a good way to remind us that God never abandons us. He will always guide and strengthen us as we trust and obey Him.

Your life will have many joyful and happy events. But there may also be times of pain and struggle. As you face these times—both pleasant and hard—use your journal to track your thoughts, prayers, fears, joys, victories, failures, and God's answers and help as you walk with Him. What you write down today becomes your memories for tomorrow. Reading and remembering how God cared for you in the past can give you strength and courage to face the challenges of today.

Your life is a one-of-a-kind adventure. "Track Your Walk" and you'll be amazed to see the fingerprints of God all over the "pages" of your life!

USING THE FEATURES IN THIS JOURNAL:

Daily Journal: Don't wait for the perfect time to begin your journal. Start today. Write as much or as little as you wish each day. Don't be discouraged if you miss a day or two. This journal is written by you, for you.

Country Prayer Points: Join thousands of other journal users praying for needy people and nations all over the world.

Track Your Month: Be careful to fill in the correct month and date. Track birthdays, school events—anything you need to remember during the month!

Prayer Tracking: Use this area to write down the people or prayer requests you want to pray for.

Scripture Memory: (See Scripture memory section)

Glossary of Terms: Use this section to look up terms you don't know. Don't skip over words you don't understand. Use the glossary or a dictionary to help you understand what you are reading.

2 Track Bible Reading Plan: Use Track One to read the New Testament and Psalms in a year. Track Two helps you read the entire Bible in a year.

I will remember the deeds of the Lord. . .
Psalm 77:11

FriEndShiP WiTh GoD

You are special. No one else is like you. God created and designed you in His image so you could know His love and have a fantastic relationship with Him. Because of sin, all people were separated from God and were unable to have a relationship with Him. The Bible says that sin leads to death. But Jesus, God's Son, died on the cross in our place. And God brought Him back to life so that if we trust our salvation to Jesus, we can know God and have His friendship forever.

The first step is to admit our sin and that we need Jesus to save us. Sin doesn't have to be something really bad like murder. It can be saying something unkind on purpose or cheating on a test. We all sin. But when we 'fess up to it and ask Jesus to save us, He spares us from the consequence of our sin.

Next, God calls us to repent, that is turn away from our old sinful way of life and walk with Him in friendship. God wants you to talk with Him. He wants you to tell Him everything in your heart. Unlike your friends on earth, God is always there for you. He will always love you . . . forever.

• **If you haven't already,** ask Jesus right now to forgive your sins so you can begin a wonderful relationship with Him. (Romans 6:23 and Romans 10:9-10)
• **Reading the Bible helps you grow** because you learn more about God and what He wants for you. (Psalm 119:11)
• **Talk to God** like you would talk to your best friend. He understands your heart and words no matter how old you are or how well you speak. (Psalm 62:8)
• **If you are tempted** and slip back into your old sinful habits, tell God whatever you did, ask His forgiveness, and then continue to walk with Him. When we confess our sin, God will always forgive us! (I John 1:9)

Now this is eternal life: that they may know you, the only true God, and Jesus Christ, whom you have sent.

John 17:3

ScRipturE MeMoriZatiOn

Memorizing Scripture is one of the most important and rewarding jobs in a Christian's life. It can also be one of the most difficult.

We may not always feel like taking the time to work on Scripture memorization. If we don't shower regularly, we will soon smell the effects. If we miss too many meals in a row, we become weak and sickly. Discipline yourself to care for and feed your spiritual self the same way you do for your physical self. Just as good food and exercise create a strong and healthy physical body, feasting regularly on God's Word will make you a spiritually strong and healthy young woman or man of God.

Throughout this journal, you'll find suggested Scriptures to memorize - approximately one for every ten days. If you successfully memorize each one, you will know 37 Scriptures by heart at the end of one year. Here are some tips to assist you as you memorize.

1) PRAY: Start by asking God to help you in the important job of memorizing His Word. Ask Him for a clear mind and the ability to concentrate.

2) READ: Repeat the passage out loud several times. It's important to ask yourself if you understand what the verse means. If you don't know the meaning of a word look it up in the dictionary or ask your parents or pastor to explain the word or passage. Memorizing something you don't understand has very little value.

3) WRITE: Copy the passage on paper several times. Focus on the meaning of the scripture, not just the words. Continue to speak or write the words until you can repeat the entire passage without looking. You may wish to keep a separate notebook to record your Scriptures. HINT: If the passage is fairly long, break it down into smaller parts and memorize each part.

4) GOALS: You are memorizing God's Word for YOUR own personal growth and benefit so set reasonable goals. If one passage every ten days is too much, adjust it to an amount you can handle. Many people quit memorizing Scripture because they set goals too high to make. Don't become discouraged if you have a break in your memorization program. Just pick up where you left off and keep going. If you miss a meal or two at the table, you don't quit eating . . . right?

5) REVIEW & USE: Finally, look back over what you memorized. Using what you have learned is important. As you continue to memorize passages, review the Scriptures you learned earlier. Use the passages you committed to memory. You will be amazed at the opportunities to encourage a friend or even yourself with the Word of God that you have hidden in your heart.

God gave His Word to teach, strengthen and guide us. So pull up a chair to the spiritual feast and dig in!

> **I** have hidden your word in my heart . . .
> Psalm 119:11

QuiEt TiMe

Set reasonable goals for your quiet time. Start small, say 10 minutes a day. If you miss a day, don't be discouraged…God is not keeping score on a chalkboard! He loves you and wants you to walk with Him in friendship. Although you can talk with God anywhere, at anytime, it is important to have regular time alone with Him. Remember, ten minutes every day is much better than an hour once a week.

There are no rules for what you should do in your Quiet Time each day. Everyone is different. Here are some ideas.

1. Read God's Word. When we read the Bible, God speaks to us and we learn more about His character and what He's doing in our lives.

2. Quiet your heart before Him. Spend time alone thinking about some of the characteristics of God: mercy, love, holiness, power, justice, and wisdom to name a few.

3. Talk to God. He loves to hear your voice. You can talk to Him about anything! Tell Him your plans or worries. Tell Him about your big test or the teacher you have a hard time with. Pray for friends, family, missionaries, nations, or anyone God brings to mind.

4. Thank Him for His care for you. All good things come from God. Tell Him thanks! Even in hard times, thank God for meeting your needs.

5. Listen to God's voice. Sit quietly and let Him speak to you in your heart. It takes time and practice to get to know God's voice. Remember: God will never tell you anything that does not agree with His written Word, the Bible.

Be still, and know that I am God.
Psalm 46:10

PRAYER FOR THE NATIONS...

Intercession is a fancy word meaning to pray for someone. Intercession is going before God in prayer on behalf of another person. Situations in people's lives or in far away countries can be changed because of prayer. In Revelation 7, God says there will be people from every nation, tribe, group and language standing before His throne in heaven. You can play a part in making this happen by praying for other people and nations. This journal has information that will help you pray with greater understanding.

Principles for Prayer & Intercession:

1. Have your Bible handy so God can speak to you through His Word. (Psalm 119:105)

2. Come to God with a clean heart, confessing your sins to Him. (Psalm 139:23-24)

3. Ask the Holy Spirit to help you pray for the right things. (Romans 8:26)

4. Give your thoughts and worries to God so you can concentrate on what God wants you to pray for. (Proverbs 3:5,6)

5. Give God praise. Thank Him for allowing you to be part of His mighty works through the power of prayer. (Psalm 150:2)

Ask of me, and I will make the nations your inheritance, the ends of the earth your possession.
Psalm 2:8

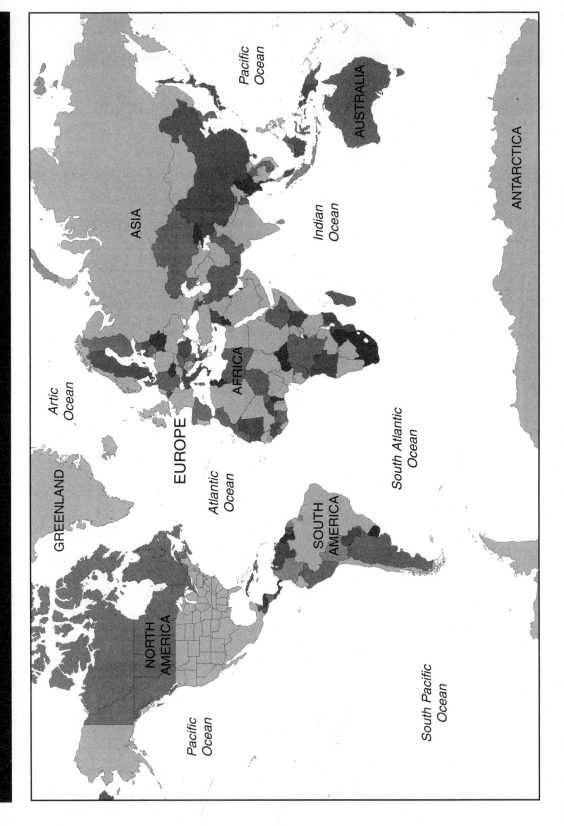

TrAcKiNG YoUr...

YEAR: 2020

MONTH: September

DAYS

SUN	MON	TUE	WED	THU	FRI	SAT
	Books at Church	1 Church Council	2	3	4	5
6	7 Labor Day	8 10 AM Dover Bank	9	10	11	12
13	14	15	16	17	18	19
20	21	22	23	24	25	26
27	28	29	30			

COLOMBIA

Colombia's Street Children

Although only about the size of Texas, almost 34 million people live in Colombia. That's twice as many people as live in the USA's Lone Star state. The streets of Bogota, the capital of Colombia, are home to thousands of children. About nine of every ten of these street kids are boys. Many use drugs and don't have jobs. While some children live with their families, they may spend most of their time on the streets working. Others live in poor slums and often end up living or working on the streets because their family cannot provide for them. The opportunity for Christians to show God's love and care by taking these children into their homes is great. These street kids need the security of a loving family and the knowledge of Jesus' love for them. Pray for Colombia's street children.

ARGENTINA

Argentina

From its northernmost point to its southernmost, Argentina stretches more than 2,300 miles. In fact, its southern tip is only 650 miles from the South Pole. Because of its size, Argentina's landscape is very diverse. Traveling across Argentina, you'd find towering mountains, flat plains, green forests, tiny villages, and large cities like its capital, Buenos Aires. On the flat, open range of the pampa, thousands of cattle are herded by the South American *gauchos* or cowboys. People in Argentina love to learn and read. *Futbol* or soccer is the country's favorite sport. Recently, many people have become Christians. These new Christians need more trained teachers and leaders who can help them continue to learn and grow. Pray for the nation of Argentina.

SoUth AmeRicA

Caribbean Sea

Kingstown ★ ★ Castries

NICARAGUA

★ St. George's

Managua ★ Bluefields
Barranquilla
San Jose ★ Panama
COSTA RICA
PANAMA

Valencia Caracas

VENEZUELA

Cucuta
Medellin

Bogota

COLOMBIA

Puerto Ayacucho

Pasto

Mitu

Georgetown

GUYANA

Paramaribo

SURINAME FRENCH
GUIANA

Cayenne

Camopi

Boa Vista

Serro Do Navio

ECUADOR

Baquerizo Moreno

Quito
Guayaquil
Cuenca

Iquitos

Talara

PERU

Chiclayo

Orellana

Trujillo

Tarauaca

Huaraz
Huanuco
Cerro De Pasco
Huancayo
Ayacucho

Lima

Ica
Cuzco

Tefe

Manaus

Santarem

Macapa

Belem

Sao Luis

Fortaleza

Sao Goncalo

Imperatriz

Teresina

Jacareacanga

Porto Velho

Cachimbo

Rio Branco

BRAZIL

Recife

Maceio

Gurupi

Barreiras

Aracaju

Alvorada

Salvador

Canavieiras

BOLIVIA

La Paz

Puno

Santa Cruz

Cuiaba

Brasilia

Goiania

Sucre

Arica

Iquique

Tarija

Belo Horizonte

Campo Grande

Vitoria

PARAGUAY

Campinas

Boa Vista

Rio De Janeiro

Antofagasta

Asuncion

Sao Paulo

Salta

CHILE

Curitiba

San Miguel De Tucuman

Florianopolis

Resistencia

Porto Alegre

Valparaiso

Santiago

Cordoba

Rosario

Tacuarembo

URUGUAY

Buenos Aires

Durazno

Montevideo

Concepcion

ARGENTINA

Mar Del Plata

Neuquen

Bahia Blanca

Valdivia

Puerto Montt

San Carlos de Bariloche

Rawson

Comodoro Rivadavia

FALKLAND ISLANDS

Puerto Santa Cruz
Rio Gallegos

Port Stanley

Ushuaia

SOUTH GEORGIA ISLAND

Go iNto AII tHe WoRLd

Go into all the world and preach the
good news to all creation.

Mark 16:15

DATE	DAILY JOURNAL

DATE	DAILY JOURNAL

TrAcKiNG YoUr...

PRAYER PRIORITIES

DATE	DAILY JOURNAL

DATE	DAILY JOURNAL

PrAisE THe LoRd

Let everything that has breath praise the Lord. Praise the Lord.

Psalm 150:6

DATE	DAILY JOURNAL

DATE	DAILY JOURNAL

TrAcKiNG YoUr...

PRAYER PRIORITIES

DATE	DAILY JOURNAL

DAiLY JoURnaL...

DATE	DAILY JOURNAL

CoMe tO Me

Come to me, all you who are weary and burdened, and I will give you rest.
Matthew 11:28

DATE	DAILY JOURNAL

DATE	DAILY JOURNAL

TrAcKiNG YoUr...

PRAYER PRIORITIES

DATE	DAILY JOURNAL

DAiLY JoURnaL...

DATE	DAILY JOURNAL

DAiLY JoURnaL...

DATE	DAILY JOURNAL

TrAcKiNG YoUr...

YEAR: _____

MONTH: _____

DAYS

SUN	MON	TUE	WED	THUR	FRI	SAT

BRAZIL

Brazil

Bigger than the 48 continental United States, Brazil is the largest country in South America. The Amazon rain forest covers much of this hot, rain-soaked country. Most of the world's coffee is grown in Brazil's mountains. Brazil is also home to thousands of different butterflies. People use their beautiful patterned wings to decorate trays and jewelry boxes. Many Brazilian kids enjoy watching and playing baseball, tennis and soccer. Sadly, Brazil like its neighbor Colombia, has many children who live on the streets without a home or a family. Many Brazilians are becoming Christians and are excited about preaching the Gospel in other lands. Currently, there are almost 2,000 missionaries from Brazil working in different countries around the world. Pray for the new Christians and the street kids in Brazil.

BOLIVIA

Bolivia

The Amazon rain forest in Bolivia is a hot, dense jungle where the rain falls all year long. The rain forest is home to a number of strange and unusual animals like the tiny, six-inch long, pygmy marmoset monkey, and the long-armed, long-tailed spider monkey. Bolivian Indians living in the jungle have to watch out for the deadly river piranha, a fish with razor sharp teeth. They also have to keep their eyes open for the giant anaconda snake, which can grow to be 24-feet long and a foot thick! However, more dangerous than any animal is the illegal drug cocaine. Half of the world's cocaine supply is grown in Bolivia. Many of Bolivia's children are neglected and are hardened by drug use and violence. Christians need to reach Bolivia's young people with God's message of love and salvation. Pray for the families of Bolivia.

SoUth AmeRicA

Caribbean Sea

Kingstown · Castries
St. George's

NICARAGUA
Managua
Bluefields
Barranquilla
Valencia · Caracas
Costa Rica
San Jose
Panama
COSTA RICA
PANAMA

VENEZUELA
Georgetown
Paramaribo
Cucuta
Medellin
GUYANA
Cayenne
Bogota
Puerto Ayacusho
SURINAME
FRENCH GUIANA
COLOMBIA
Boa Vista
Camopi
Pasto
Mitu
Serro Do Navio
ECUADOR
Quito
Macapa
Baquerizo Moreno
Guayaquil
Cuenca
Belem
Sao Luis
Manaus
Santarem
Fortaleza
Talara
Tefe
Iquitos
PERU
Jacareacanga
Sao Goncalo
Teresina
Chiclayo
Orellana
Imperatriz
Recife
Trujillo
Tarauaca
Porto Velho
Cachimbo
Maceio
Huaraz
Rio Branco
Aracaju
Huanuco
BRAZIL
Gurupi
Barreiras
Cerro De Pasco
Alvorada
Salvador
Huancayo
Canavieiras
Lima
Ayacucho
Cuzco
Ica
BOLIVIA
Brasilia
Puno
La Paz
Cuiaba
Goiania
Arica
Sucre
Santa Cruz
Belo Horizonte
Iquique
Tarija
Campo Grande
Vitoria
Antofagasta
PARAGUAY
Boa Vista
Campinas
Rio De Janeiro
Salta
Asuncion
Sao Paulo
CHILE
San Miguel De Tucuman
Curitiba
Resistencia
Florianopolis
Cordoba
Tacuarembo
Porto Alegre
Valparaiso
Santiago
Rosario
URUGUAY
Concepcion
Buenos Aires
Durazno
Valdivia
ARGENTINA
Montevideo
Neuquen
Bahia Blanca
Mar Del Plata
Puerto Montt
San Carlos de Bariloche
Rawson
Comodoro Rivadavia

Puerto Santa Cruz
Rio Gallegos
FALKLAND ISLANDS
Ushuaia
Port Stanley

SOUTH GEORGIA ISLAND

Do wHAt It SayS

Do not merely listen to the word,
and so deceive yourselves. Do what
it says.

James 1:22

DATE	DAILY JOURNAL

DAiLY JoURnaL...

DATE	DAILY JOURNAL

PRAYER PRIORITIES

DATE	DAILY JOURNAL

DAiLY JoURnaL...

DATE	DAILY JOURNAL

I Can dO EveRyThiNg

I can do everything through him who gives me strength.

Philippians 4:13

DATE	DAILY JOURNAL

DAiLY JoURnaL...

DATE	DAILY JOURNAL

PRAYER PRIORITIES

DATE	DAILY JOURNAL

DAiLY JoURnaL...

DATE	DAILY JOURNAL

God made him who had no sin to be
sin for us, so that in him we might
become the righteousness of God.
                    II Corinthians 5:21

DATE	DAILY

DAiLY JoURnaL...

DATE	DAILY JOURNAL

PRAYER PRIORITIES

DATE	DAILY JOURNAL

DAiLY JoURnaL...

DATE	DAILY JOURNAL

DAiLY JoURnaL...

DATE	DAILY JOURNAL

YEAR:

MONTH:

DAYS

SUN	MON	TUE	WED	THUR	FRI	SAT

GREECE

Greece

If you traveled to Athens, Greece you'd see some of the world's oldest ruins. Almost 3,000 years ago, athletes met at Olympia to compete in the first Olympic Games. Just like their ancestors, many coastal villagers still earn their living catching crab, octopus or fish. In school, students study the Eastern Orthodox faith. The normal school day ends at just past noon. Greece was the first European country to hear the good news of the Gospel (Acts 16:10). While there are many churches in Greece today, few people regularly attend. The official Greek church sees witnessing about Jesus as a threat. In fact, Christians can still be persecuted or jailed for sharing about the Lord. Some Greek homes have a small family chapel with the names of dead family members written on the walls and their bones kept inside. Pray for the people of Greece.

MOROCCO

Morocco

Located on the northeastern coast of Africa, Morocco means "Land of the Setting Sun". Tourists come to sunbathe on the ocean beaches and explore the colorful bazaars. Able to survive several days without water, camels often haul goods or transport people in this warm, dry country. Children attend school, but often dropout early to work full-time. Ninety-nine of every hundred Moroccans are Muslims. Five times daily, Muslim worshippers face the city of Mecca, bow face down on a prayer rug, and recite verses from the Koran. Eighty percent of the people have never heard the gospel. Moroccan Christians are persecuted for their faith. Harassment, loss of jobs, or prison can be the fate of anyone who openly shares about Jesus. Christians gather in small, secret meetings so churches as we know them do not exist. Pray for the nation of Morocco. (See map - page 61)

EuRopE

The grass withers and the flowers fall, but the word of our God stands forever.

Isaiah 40:8

DATE	DAILY JOURNAL

DAiLY JoURnaL...

DATE	DAILY JOURNAL

PRAYER PRIORITIES

_____
_____
_____
_____

DATE	DAILY JOURNAL

DAiLY JoURnaL...

DATE	DAILY JOURNAL

Have I not commanded you? Be strong
and courageous. Do not be terrified; do
not be discouraged, for the Lord your
God will be with you wherever you go.
Joshua 1:9

DATE	DAILY JOURNAL

DAiLY JoURnaL...

DATE	DAILY JOURNAL

PRAYER PRIORITIES

DATE	DAILY JOURNAL

DAiLY JoURnaL...

DATE	DAILY JOURNAL

DeClaRe HiS GlOry

Declare his glory among the nations,
his marvelous deeds among all peoples.
Psalm 96:3

DATE	DAILY JOURNAL

DAiLY JoURnaL...

DATE	DAILY JOURNAL

PRAYER PRIORITIES

DATE	DAILY JOURNAL

DAiLY JoURnaL...

DATE	DAILY JOURNAL

DAiLY JoURnaL...

DATE	DAILY JOURNAL

TrAcKiNG YoUr...

YEAR: _____

MONTH: _____

Days

SUN	MON	TUE	WED	THUR	FRI	SAT

KENYA

Kenya

The wildlife reserves in Kenya are world famous. Zebras, lions, giraffes, and many beautiful birds are protected in these large reserves. The world's fastest animal, the cheetah, lives in Kenya. The Masai people, one of 27 tribes in Kenya, spend much of their time tending their cattle. The women love to decorate themselves with large earrings and many beads. The men have long, thick hair. Masai children wear leather clothes and jingling bracelets on their wrists. Masai people are known for their white teeth, and greatly enjoy their favorite drink, a mixture of cow's blood and milk. There is great freedom to preach the Gospel in Kenya. Although many Kenyans are Christians, few attend church. Lately, interest in missions has increased among Kenyans. Over 500 missionaries travel from Kenya to other tribes and countries to share the Gospel. Pray for the nation of Kenya.

ETHIOPIA

Ethiopia

Ethiopia is probably one of the oldest nations on earth. There are over sixty references to this African country in the Bible. As in ancient times, farming and herding is a way of life in Ethiopia. When boys reach eight years of age, they become the main shepherd in the family. By the time they reach eighteen, each boy hopes to have mastered the skills to become a warrior. To do so, boys test each other's bravery and play games that will help them develop warrior skills. Ethiopia's people have been through much heartache from disease, wars and lack of rain and food. Less than twenty percent of Ethiopians can read or write. Some Ethiopians combine Christian beliefs with a traditional belief in the power of nature. All of these troubles make for great sadness and despair in Ethiopia. Pray for God's grace for the people of Ethiopia.

AfricA

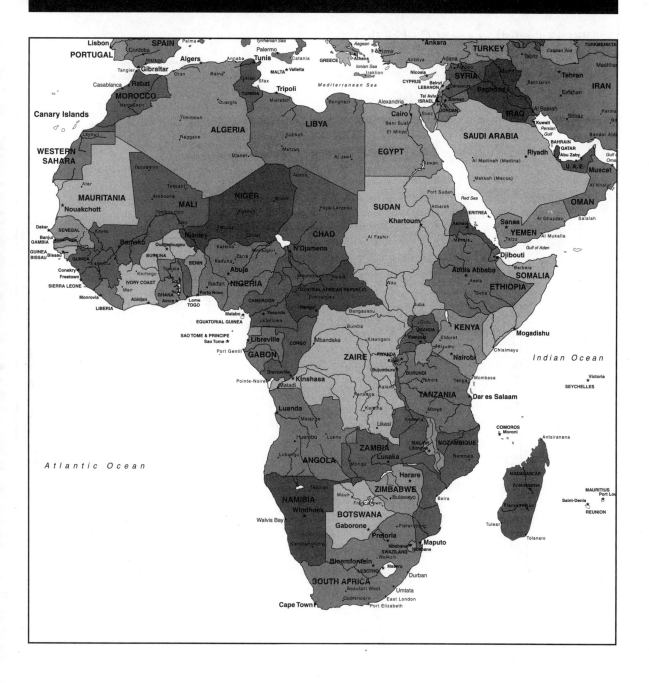

Put on the full armor of God so that you can take your stand against the devil's schemes.

Ephesians 6:11

DATE	DAILY JOURNAL

DAiLY JoURnaL...

DATE	DAILY JOURNAL

PRAYER PRIORITIES

DATE	DAILY JOURNAL

DATE	DAILY JOURNAL

BuT WhEn You aRe TempTed

But when you are tempted, he will also provide a way out so that you can stand up under it.

I Corinthians 10:13b

DATE	DAILY JOURNAL

DAiLY JoURnaL...

DATE	DAILY JOURNAL

PRAYER PRIORITIES

_____
_____
_____
_____

DATE	DAILY JOURNAL

DAiLY JoURnaL...

DATE	DAILY JOURNAL

FruiT Of ThE SpiRiT

But the fruit of the Spirit is love, joy, peace, patience, kindness, goodness, faithfulness, gentleness and self-control. Against such things there is no law.

Galatians 5:22, 23

DATE	DAILY JOURNAL

DAiLY JoURnaL...

DATE	DAILY JOURNAL

TrAcKiNG YoUr...

PRAYER PRIORITIES

DATE	DAILY JOURNAL

DAiLY JoURnaL...

DATE	DAILY JOURNAL

DAiLY JoURnaL...

DATE	DAILY JOURNAL

TrAcKiNG YoUr...

YEAR:

MONTH:

DAYS

SUN	MON	TUE	WED	THUR	FRI	SAT

CANADA

Canada

Larger than the United States, Canada is a nation with two official languages. People in Quebec, an eastern province, speak French. The rest of Canada mainly speaks English. This has contributed to tension in Canada. Many who live in Quebec desire their province to become a separate nation from Canada. One point most Canadians agree upon is their love for ice hockey, the national sport. Western Canada is home to beautiful Banff and Jasper National Parks where you can travel over huge glaciers on a special bus. Most Canadians consider themselves Christians, yet fewer and fewer people are going to church. Among Native Canadian Indians, there is a great need for churches to preach the gospel. Large groups of Sikhs, Muslims and Hindus live in Canada's cities. They also need to hear about Jesus. Pray for the nation of Canada.

USA

United States of America

Called the great melting pot, the United States is home to people from almost every nation on earth. America sends out many missionaries to other nations, but today the United States itself is a huge mission field. Americans' beliefs about God are as varied as the people themselves. From atheism to New Age beliefs, almost every religion is practiced. Although it has long been considered the leader of the free world and has been greatly blessed by God, this rich and powerful nation has deep troubles. Racial tension, crowded cities, and violent crime are of great concern. Many families don't have both parents living at home, and often biblical values are no longer practiced. This has left deep scars on this complex society. Many young people are overwhelmed with options while others drift along without purpose or direction for their life. Pray for the United States of America.

Whatever you do, work at it with all your heart, as working for the Lord, not for men.

Colossians 3:23

DATE	DAILY JOURNAL

DATE	DAILY JOURNAL

PRAYER PRIORITIES

DATE	DAILY JOURNAL

DAiLY JoURnaL...

DATE	DAILY JOURNAL

Be KiNd and ComPasSiOnatE

Be kind and compassionate to one
another, forgiving each other, just as in
Christ God forgave you.

Ephesians 4:32

DATE	DAILY JOURNAL

DAiLY JoURnaL...

DATE	DAILY JOURNAL

PRAYER PRIORITIES

DATE	DAILY JOURNAL

DAiLY JoURnaL...

DATE	DAILY JOURNAL

The HeaVEns DecLarE

The heavens declare the glory of God;
the skies proclaim the work of his
hands.

                    Psalm 19:1

DATE	DAILY JOURNAL

DAiLY JoURnaL...

DATE	DAILY JOURNAL

PRAYER PRIORITIES

DATE	DAILY JOURNAL

DAiLY JoURnaL...

DATE	DAILY JOURNAL

DATE	DAILY JOURNAL

TrAcKiNG YoUr...

YEAR: _____

MONTH: _____

Days

SUN	MON	TUE	WED	THUR	FRI	SAT

ESKIMOS

Eskimo People

Eskimo people call themselves *Inupiaq* (in-OO-pee-ak) or "the real people". You'll find them living in Greenland, Alaska and Northern Canada. Most Eskimos are hunters and fisherman who live in regular houses, not igloos. Today, snowmobiles have replaced most dogsleds. In winter, Eskimos live almost two months without seeing the sun. In the summer, the sun shines day and night. Life for the Eskimo can be hard, so children are encouraged to play and have fun while they are young. Parents are careful to teach their children how to survive in their harsh climate by fishing, hunting, making igloos, and sewing furs or leather for clothing. Missionaries have brought the Gospel to the Eskimos, but a modern lifestyle has destroyed the purpose for living for many people. The suicide rate is very high among the Eskimos. Pray for the Eskimo people.

PUEBLO INDIANS

Pueblo Indians in the USA

The Pueblo Indians live in north central Arizona and New Mexico. *Pueblo* (PWEH-bloh) means small town in Spanish. Early Pueblo Indians built their homes like apartment houses, one on top of another. Pueblo children are well-behaved and seldom need to be punished. You might see them playing tug-of-war or stick ball. When boys reach age twelve, they can enter the sacred *Kiva*, a round room that is mostly underground. The men hold secret meetings in the Kiva and teach songs and dances they hope will cure the sick and make the rain fall. At a young age, girls learn to make pottery and help their mothers with chores. Most Pueblo Indians worship a Mother Earth and a Father Sky. Some Pueblo Indians are Christians, but most worship only their ancient gods. Others try to follow Christ and worship ancient gods at the same time. Pray for the Pueblo Indians.

NorTh AmeRicA

AsK...SeeK...KnocK

Ask and it will be given to you; seek
and you will find; knock and the
door will be opened to you.

Matthew 7:7

DATE	DAILY JOURNAL

DAiLY JoURnaL...

DATE	DAILY JOURNAL

PRAYER PRIORITIES

DATE	DAILY JOURNAL

DAiLY JoURnaL...

DATE	DAILY JOURNAL

But you are a shield around me, O Lord; you bestow glory on me and lift up my head.

Psalm 3:3

DATE	DAILY JOURNAL

DATE	DAILY JOURNAL

PRAYER PRIORITIES

DATE	DAILY JOURNAL

DAiLY JoURnaL...

DATE	DAILY JOURNAL

LoVe tHe LoRd

Love the Lord your God will all your
heart and with all your soul and with
all your strength.

Deuteronomy 6:5

DATE	DAILY JOURNAL

DAiLY JoURnaL...

DATE	DAILY JOURNAL

TrAcKiNG YoUr...

PRAYER PRIORITIES

DATE	DAILY JOURNAL

DAiLY JoURnaL...

DATE	DAILY JOURNAL

DAiLY JoURnaL...

DAILY JOURNAL

DATE	

TrAcKiNG YoUr...

YEAR:

MONTH:

DaYS

SUN	MON	TUE	WED	THUR	FRI	SAT

Most people who haven't heard the Gospel live in a window! This window is a rectangle-shaped area that extends from West Africa across Asia, between ten and forty degrees north of the equator. Our prayers and efforts need to be focused on this 10/40 Window. Millions of people need to hear about the love of God and His plan of salvation through Jesus Christ.

FACTS ABOUT THE 10/40 WINDOW...

Three large religious groups are located in the 10/40 Window: Muslims, Hindus, and Buddhists. The poorest people in the world live in this region. Over half of the world's people live in poverty with an average income of just $500 (US) per year per person. Only eight percent of all missionaries work in the 10/40 Window. The top fifty percent of the world's least evangelized cities are all located in the 10/40 Window. All fifty of these cities have more than one million people living in them. Pray for the hundreds of millions of people in the 10/40 Window who have suffered poverty and disease and have been kept from the power of the Gospel. Pray that Christians and missionaries will commit to reaching the 10/40 Window with the love of Jesus Christ.

COUNTRIES IN THE 10/40 WINDOW

Afghanistan	Djibouti	Iran	Macau	Portugal	Turkmenistan
Algeria	Egypt *	Iraq	Mali	Qatar	United Arab
Bahrain	Ethiopia *	Israel	Malta	Saudi Arabia	Emirates
Bangladesh	Gambia	Japan	Mauritania	Senegal	Vietnam
Benin	Gaza Strip	Jordan	Morocco *	Sudan	West Bank
Bhutan	Gibraltar	Korea, North	Myanmar	Syria	Western Sahara
Burkina Faso	Greece *	Korea, South	Nepal	Taiwan	Yemen
Cambodia	Guinea	Kuwait	Niger	Tajikistan	
Chad	Guinea-Bissau	Laos	Oman	Thailand	*Countries
China*	Hong Kong	Lebanon	Pakistan	Tunisia	highlighted in
Cyprus	India *	Libya	Philippines	Turkey	this journal.

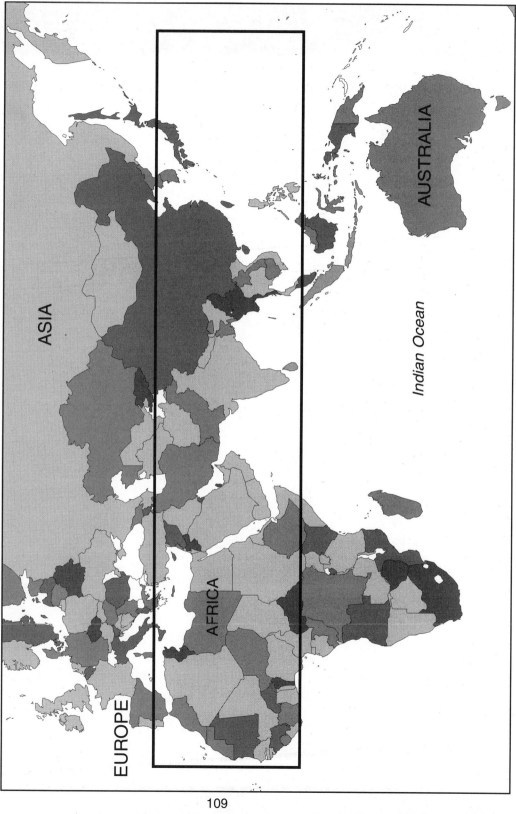

ThE 10 / 40 WinDoW

ASIA

EUROPE

AFRICA

AUSTRALIA

Indian Ocean

You aRe ThE LiGht of tHe WoRLd

You are the light of the world.
Matthew 5:14

DATE	DAILY JOURNAL

DAiLY JoURnaL...

DATE	DAILY JOURNAL

PRAYER PRIORITIES

DATE	DAILY JOURNAL

DAiLY JoURnaL...

DATE	DAILY JOURNAL

The Lord will fulfill his purpose for me;
your love, O Lord, endures forever—do
not abandon the works of your hands.

Psalm 138:8

DATE	DAILY JOURNAL

DATE	DAILY JOURNAL

PRAYER PRIORITIES

DATE	DAILY JOURNAL

DAiLY JoURnaL...

DATE	DAILY JOURNAL

HumBle YouRSeLvEs

Humble yourselves, therefore, under God's mighty hand, that he may lift you up in due time.

1 Peter 5:6

DATE	DAILY JOURNAL

DAiLY JoURnaL...

DATE	DAILY JOURNAL

PRAYER PRIORITIES

DATE	DAILY JOURNAL

DAiLY JoURnaL...

DATE	DAILY JOURNAL

DAiLY JoURnaL...

DATE	DAILY JOURNAL

YEAR:

DAYS

MONTH:

SUN	MON	TUE	WED	THUR	FRI	SAT

AUSTRALIA

Australia

The only nation that takes up an entire continent, Australia is south of the equator and is called "The Land Down Under". The four seasons are at the opposite time from countries like Canada, which is north of the equator. Winter in the United States is Australia's summer. Most Australians live in cities near the coast. In central Australia homes are so far apart that children attend the "School in the Air". School books are mailed to children by teachers, and classes are held over two-way radio. Students use their radios to ask their teacher questions. Australia's first inhabitants, the Aborigines, are famous for their skills in finding lost people. Most Australians have heard the Gospel, but many do not see God and the Bible as important to their lives. So few people go to church or support missions. Pray for the nation of Australia.

FIJI

Fiji

Fiji is made up of 332 islands in the Pacific Ocean. Two main groups of people live in Fiji: the native Fijian people and people who originally came from India. Indian Fijians are mostly Hindu or Muslim. Age is very important in a Fiji family. Young people are expected to obey and respect their elders. In turn, older people must protect and care for the young. The oldest member of the family is always served first at mealtimes. An ancient custom still in use today is drinking *Yaqona* (Yang-GON-a). Sharing a bowl of Yaqona with friends or visitors creates a bond between the participants. Fijians first received the Gospel over a hundred years ago. Today, Christianity is part of the culture, but many do not personally know Jesus as Savior. Alcohol abuse and broken families are major problems in this beautiful country. Pray for the people of Fiji.

Pacific Region

I lift up my eyes to the hills - where does my help come from? My help comes from the Lord, the Maker of heaven and earth.

Psalm 121:1,2

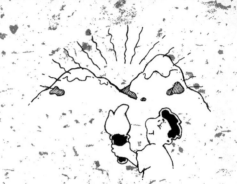

DATE	DAILY JOURNAL

DAiLY JoURnaL...

DATE	DAILY JOURNAL

PRAYER PRIORITIES

DATE	DAILY JOURNAL

DAiLY JoURnaL...

DATE	DAILY JOURNAL

A NeW CrEatiOn

Therefore, if anyone is in Christ, he is a
new creation; the old has gone, the new
has come!

II Corinthians 5:17

DATE	DAILY JOURNAL

DAiLY JoURnaL...

DATE	DAILY JOURNAL

PRAYER PRIORITIES

DATE	DAILY JOURNAL

DAiLY JoURnaL...

DATE	DAILY JOURNAL

I aM nOt AshameD

I am not ashamed of the gospel,
because it is the power of God for the
salvation of everyone who believes:
first for the Jew, then for the Gentile.

Romans 1:16

DATE	DAILY JOURNAL

DAiLY JoURnaL...

DATE	DAILY JOURNAL

PRAYER PRIORITIES

DATE	DAILY JOURNAL

DAiLY JoURnaL...

DATE	DAILY JOURNAL

DAiLY JoURnaL...

DAILY JOURNAL

DATE	

YEAR: _____

MONTH: _____

DAYS

SUN	MON	TUE	WED	THUR	FRI	SAT

MEXICO

Mexico

Most Mexicans love fiesta celebrations filled with dancing, folk music, fireworks and colorful costumes. Bullfighting is also very popular in Mexico. The largest bullfighting ring in the world is in Mexico City. In Mexican culture, families are very important, often working together in small businesses. Afternoons are very warm, so everyone goes home for a *siesta*, a time to nap or relax. In the countryside, farm boys help their fathers pick fruit from cocoa trees. Beans from this fruit are used to make delicious chocolate. Almost all Mexicans are Catholic, but in the villages Catholic beliefs are mixed with superstition, magic and worship of other gods. In Mexico City alone, 500,000 children roam the streets trying to earn money selling chewing gum or shining shoes. There is a great need for Christians to help these children. Pray for the nation of Mexico.
(See map on page 157)

CUBA

Cuba

Cuba is an island nation of about eleven million people. The excellent climate, beautiful beaches and mountain scenery attract many tourists from all over the world who also enjoy watching Cuba's well-known Afro-Spanish dancing. Various hummingbirds, including the world's smallest that measures only two-and-a-quarter inches in length, can be found all over the country. Few Cubans have had any real contact with Christianity. Christians are persecuted and often imprisoned by the government. Recently, new laws have been passed to give people more freedom to worship God. Christians can now hold meetings in homes. This is helping to increase the number of house churches, which now have permission to print and distribute books and materials. However, Bibles are still hard to find and visiting Christians are not allowed to do any public preaching. Pray for the people of Cuba.

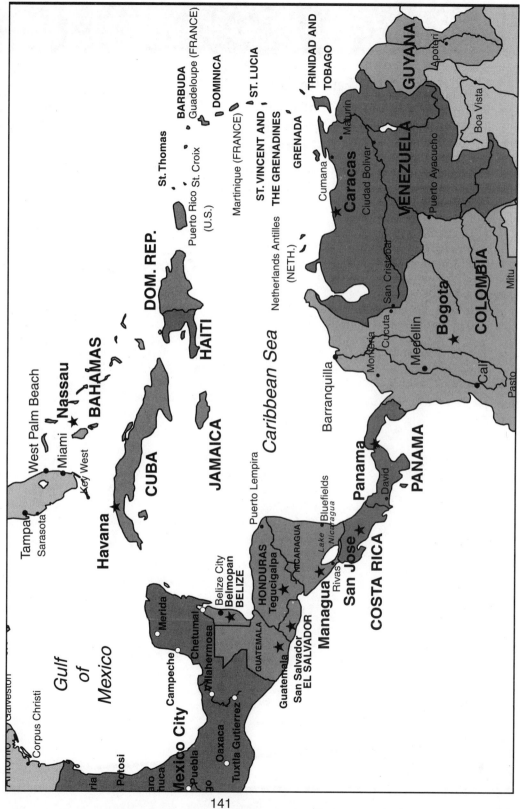

CenTraL AmERicA

Corpus Christi

Gulf of Mexico

Tampa
Sarasota

West Palm Beach
Miami
Key West

Nassau
BAHAMAS

Potosi
Puebla
Oaxaca
Tuxtla Gutierrez
Mexico City

Merida
Campeche
Chetumal
Villahermosa

CUBA

Havana

DOM. REP.

HAITI

JAMAICA

St. Thomas

Puerto Rico St. Croix
(U.S.)

BARBUDA
Guadeloupe (FRANCE)
DOMINICA
Martinique (FRANCE)
ST. LUCIA
ST. VINCENT AND
THE GRENADINES
GRENADA

TRINIDAD AND TOBAGO

Caribbean Sea

Netherlands Antilles
(NETH.)

Maturin
Caracas
Ciudad Bolivar

Cumana

VENEZUELA

Puerto Ayacucho

Boa Vista

Apoteri

GUYANA

Barranquilla

Cucuta
San Cristobal

Medellin

Monteria

Cali

Pasto

Bogota

COLOMBIA

Mitu

Belize City
Belmopan
BELIZE

HONDURAS
Tegucigalpa

Puerto Lempira

GUATEMALA

Guatemala

San Salvador
EL SALVADOR

NICARAGUA

Lake Nicaragua
Bluefields

Rivas

Managua

San Jose

COSTA RICA

David

Panama
PANAMA

141

WoNdeRfuLLy MadE

I praise you because I am fearfully
and wonderfully made; your works
are wonderful, I know that full well.
                                Psalm 139:14

DATE	DAILY JOURNAL

DAiLY JoURnaL...

DATE	DAILY JOURNAL

PRAYER PRIORITIES

DATE	DAILY JOURNAL

DAiLY JoURnaL...

DATE	DAILY JOURNAL

HonoR...FatHer aNd MoTheR

Honor your father and mother - which is the first commandment with a promise.

Ephesians 6:2

DATE	DAILY JOURNAL

DATE	DAILY JOURNAL

TrAcKiNG YoUr...

PRAYER PRIORITIES

DATE	DAILY JOURNAL

DAiLY JoURnaL...

DATE	DAILY JOURNAL

You HaVe TauGht Me

Since my youth, O God, you have taught me, and to this day I declare your marvelous deeds.

Psalm 71:17

DATE	DAILY JOURNAL

DAiLY JoURnaL...

DATE	DAILY JOURNAL

TrAcKiNG YoUr...

PRAYER PRIORITIES

DATE	DAILY JOURNAL

DAiLY JoURnaL...

DATE	DAILY JOURNAL

DAILY JoURnaL...

DAILY JOURNAL

DATE	

TrAcKiNG YoUr....

YEAR: _____

MONTH: _____

DAYS

SUN	MON	TUE	WED	THUR	FRI	SAT

HARE INDIANS

Hare Indians of Canada

The Hare Indians live in the arctic forests of northern Canada, one of the world's harshest places. Some Hare still live off the land, hunting and fishing as they have for centuries. The Hare get their name from their dependence on snowshoe hares (rabbits) for clothes and food. Clothes and blankets made from rabbit skins or pelts provide them with warmth during the cold winters. Today, many Hare Indians work regular jobs, but make extra money fur trapping. Finding food to eat and simply staying alive have always been a great concern of the Hare. They often turn to religion as a way of dealing with their hard life. As the Hare begin to settle in towns, their way of life is rapidly changing. Adjusting to a new lifestyle has left many Hare young people confused about who they are and uncertain of their Indian traditions. Pray for the Hare Indians.

INTER- NATIONAL STUDENTS

International Students in the USA

American Christians have a mission field in their own backyard! Almost 500,000 students from other countries come to the United States to attend school. Most speak English, are eager to learn new things, and often want to make new friends. Many come from countries that do not allow people to share about Christianity. Studying in the United States may be the first chance many have to hear about Jesus. These students are often some of the brightest, most talented young people in their nation. After returning home, they may be placed in positions of leadership that will affect their entire country. This is a great opportunity to make friends with someone who might never have heard the Gospel. Through friendship and sharing the Gospel with one student, an entire country might be changed. Pray for the International Students in the USA

YouR WoRd iS a LamP

Your word is a lamp to my feet and a light for my path.

Psalm 119:105

DATE	DAILY JOURNAL

DATE	DAILY JOURNAL

PRAYER PRIORITIES

_____
_____
_____
_____

DATE	DAILY JOURNAL

DAiLY JoURnaL...

DATE	DAILY JOURNAL

I remember the days of long ago; I meditate on all your works and consider what your hands have done.

Psalm 143:5

DATE	DAILY JOURNAL

DAiLY JoURnaL...

DATE	DAILY JOURNAL

TrAcKiNG YoUr...

PRAYER PRIORITIES

DATE	DAILY JOURNAL

DAiLY JoURnaL...

DATE	DAILY JOURNAL

The Gift Of God

For the wages of sin is death, but the gift of God is eternal life in Christ Jesus our Lord.

Romans 6:23

DATE	DAILY JOURNAL

DAiLY JoURnaL...

DATE	DAILY JOURNAL

PRAYER PRIORITIES

DATE	DAILY JOURNAL

DAILY JoURnaL...

DATE	DAILY JOURNAL

DATE	DAILY JOURNAL

TrAcKiNG YoUr...

MONTH:

YEAR:

DAYS

SUN	MON	TUE	WED	THUR	FRI	SAT

PrAYiNG For...

EGYPT

Egypt

Egypt is an ancient land that today is home to almost 60 million people. Moses lead the Israelites out of Egypt almost 3,500 years ago. The pyramids were built long before the birth of Christ as giant tombs for Egyptian rulers. No one is certain exactly how these great structures were built without modern construction equipment. Because most of Egypt is desert, only a small amount of land along the Nile River can be farmed. Many of the ten million people living in Cairo, the capital city, are very poor. Schools are very crowded, so students only attend classes half days. Islam is the official religion of Egypt. Some Muslims who become Christians may be imprisoned or killed, and fear and persecution is turning others back to Islam. Most Muslims in Egypt have never personally heard about Jesus from a Christian. Many Egyptian churches have no pastor. Pray for the nation of Egypt.

RUSSIA

Russia: C.I.S.

Russia is almost as large as all of South America. The land ranges from warm beaches to icy tundra. During Russia's long, cold winters kids enjoy ice skating and playing in the snow. Reindeer racing is popular in the frozen north. For seventy years, the communist rulers of Russia did not allow religion to be taught or practiced. The prayers of many Christians played a part in seeing religious freedom become possible in 1990 and 1991. Right now many Russians are very open to the Gospel. Russia's schools and government are now allowing the Bible to be taught and used. But there are still many people in Russia who haven't heard about Jesus, especially in rural areas like Siberia. False religions and cults are also entering Russia, and some people are getting confused about the true message of salvation. Pray for the Russian people.

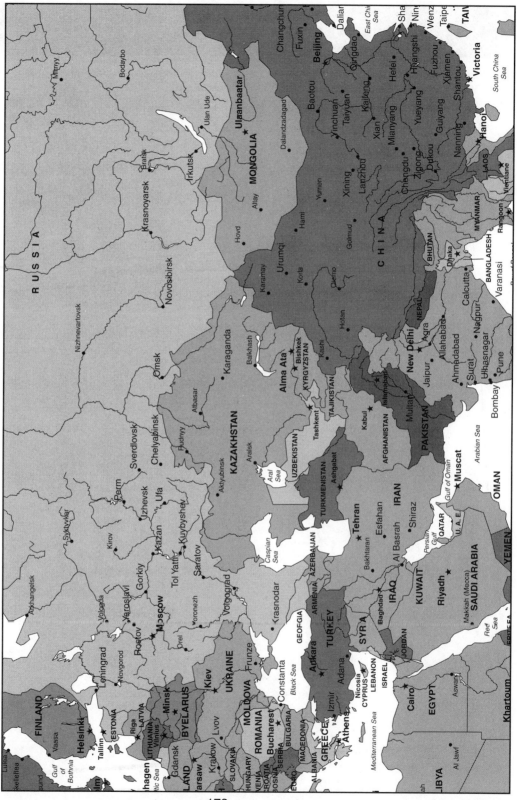

CenTraL AsiA

Even youths grow tired and weary, and young men stumble and fall; but those who hope in the Lord will renew their strength.

Isaiah 40:30,31a

DATE	DAILY JOURNAL

DATE	DAILY JOURNAL

TrAcKiNG YoUr...

PRAYER PRIORITIES

DATE	DAILY JOURNAL

DAiLY JoURnaL...

DATE	DAILY JOURNAL

I WiLL iNsTrucT YoU

I will instruct you and teach you in the
way you should go; I will counsel you
and watch over you.

Psalm 32:8

DATE	DAILY JOURNAL

DAiLY JoURnaL...

DATE	DAILY JOURNAL

PRAYER PRIORITIES

_____

_____

_____

_____

DATE	DAILY JOURNAL

DAILY JOURNAL...

DATE	DAILY JOURNAL

Trust in the Lord with all your heart
and lean not on your own understanding; in all your ways acknowledge him,
and he will make your paths straight.

Proverbs 3:5,6

DATE	DAILY JOURNAL

DAiLY JoURnaL...

DATE	DAILY JOURNAL

PRAYER PRIORITIES

DATE	DAILY JOURNAL

DAiLY JoURnaL...

DATE	DAILY JOURNAL

DATE	DAILY JOURNAL

TrAcKiNG YoUr...

YEAR: _____

MONTH: _____

DAYS

SUN	MON	TUE	WED	THUR	FRI	SAT

CHINA

China

More people live in China than in any country on earth. China's government controls most people's daily life. School is very important in China. Classes begin at 7:00 a.m. and don't end until 5:00 p.m. Then students go home to a long evening of homework. While students hope to go to university, space is limited and few can attend. The country's leaders forbid the 500 million people under 18 to even hear the Gospel. Missionaries are not welcome and Christians may be persecuted. Still, the number of Christians is growing very fast. Some people estimate there are 30 - 75 million Christians in China. Even though more than a million Bibles are printed in China each year, they are very hard to get. This is far too few for the many millions of Chinese Christians who have no Bible. Pray for the people of China.

CHILD LABORERS IN INDIA

India's Child Laborers

More than 850 million people live in India. Millions of Indians are very poor. As a result, more than 40 million children under fourteen are forced to work. These children do not mow lawns or deliver papers. Instead they have difficult and dangerous jobs like surfacing roads or working in glass, fireworks and garment factories. Their workday can be twelve hours long, and a normal workweek is six or seven days. Their weekly pay is equal to only $1.25 (US dollars). Sometimes children are injured at work. They may get severely burned or cut from broken glass. Most kids are not able to attend school, and never learn to read and write. These children have little hope for escape from this difficult life of labor. They desperately need the lasting hope that Jesus can provide. Pray for the child laborers in India.

The LeaSt oF TheSe

I tell you the truth, whatever you did
for one of the least of these brothers
of mine, you did for me.

Matthew 25:40

DATE	DAILY JOURNAL

DAiLY JoURnaL...

DATE	DAILY JOURNAL

TrAcKiNG YoUr...

PRAYER PRIORITIES

DATE	DAILY JOURNAL

DAILY JoURnaL...

DATE	DAILY JOURNAL

GoD iS ouR rEfuGe

Trust in him at all times, O people;
pour out your hearts to him, for God is
our refuge.

Psalm 62:8

DATE	DAILY JOURNAL

DAILY JoURnaL...

DATE	DAILY JOURNAL

PRAYER PRIORITIES

DATE	DAILY JOURNAL

DAiLY JoURnaL...

DATE	DAILY JOURNAL

Go aNd MakE DisCipLes

Therefore go and make disciples of all nations, baptizing them in the name of the Father and of the Son and of the Holy Spirit.

Matthew 28:19

DATE	DAILY JOURNAL

DAiLY JoURnaL...

DATE	DAILY JOURNAL

PRAYER PRIORITIES

DATE	DAILY JOURNAL

DAiLY JoURnaL...

DATE	DAILY JOURNAL

PerfEcT PeaCe

You will keep in perfect peace him whose mind is steadfast, because he trusts in you.

Isaiah 26:3

DATE	DAILY JOURNAL

DAiLY JoURnaL...

DATE	DAILY JOURNAL

FACTS & PRAYER POINTS

Argentina - South America
Population: 34,264,000
Capital: Buenos Aires
Language: Spanish
Christian: 95.5% (Evangelicals: 6.9%)
Muslim: 1.5%
Pray for:
- The revival of Christianity in Argentina to continue until it reaches even the most remote parts of the country.
- More Christian leaders and pastors to disciple the growing number of Christians.

Australia - Pacific
Population: 17,690,000
Capital: Canberra
Language: English
Christian: 70.6% (Evangelicals: 12.6%)
Muslim: 1.5%
Secular: 26.6%
Pray for:
- The nearly 500 missionaries working among the Aborigines.
- The hearts of the Aborigines, and all Australians, to be open to the Gospel.

Bolivia - South America
Population: 8,421,000
Capital: La Paz
Language: Spanish, Quechua, Aymara
Christian: 75.7% (Evangelicals: 8.4%)
Animist: 15%
Secular: 5.9%
Pray for:
- An end to production of the dangerous drug, cocaine.
- Christians to reach out in love to the neglected youth of Bolivia.

Brazil - South America
Population: 165,083,000
Capital: Brasilia
Language: Portuguese
Christian: 92.4% (Evangelicals: 17.8%)
Animist: 4.8%
Secular: 2.4%
Pray for:
- The eight million children who are living on the streets or in the sewers of Brazil's cities.
- More Christian leaders and pastors to teach and disciple the many new Christians.

Canada - North America
Population: 27,567,000
Capital: Ottawa

Language: English, French
Christian 83.5% (Evangelicals: 7.7%)
Secular: 12.1%
Pray for:
- Revival in this vast nation that is home to people from so many different countries.
- More churches that believe and teach the Bible to be started among the Canadian Indians.

China - Northern Asia
Population: 1,214,221,000
Capital: Beijing
Language: Mandarin Chinese, others
Christian: 6.1% (Evangelicals: 5%)
Muslim: 2.4%
Buddhist: 30%
Animist: 2.4%
Secular: 59.1%
Pray for:
- The millions of people in China who have not yet heard the Gospel message.
- More Bibles for the millions of Chinese who desperately want and need them.

Colombia - South America
Population: 34,939,000
Capital: Bogota
Language: Spanish
Christian: 97.5% (Evangelicals: 3.1%)
Secular: 1.6%
Pray for:
- More Christians who want to work with street kids and children in the slums.
- Protection for the street children living in the midst of crime and violence.

Cuba - Caribbean
Population: 10,788,000
Capital: Havana
Language: Spanish
Christian: 44.1% (Evangelicals: 2.54%)
Animist: 25%
Secular: 30.9%
Pray for:
- Greater freedom to worship and preach openly for Christians in Cuba.
- Political freedom for this nation under the rule of communism.
- More Bibles for those who desire to read God's Word.

Egypt - North Africa
Population: 60,470,000
Capital: Cairo
Language: Arabic
Christian: 14.2% (Evangelicals: 0.73%)
Muslim: 85.4%
Pray for:
- More pastors to train and disciple the Egyptian Christians.
- Open hearts among Muslims to hear and respond to the message of salvation.
- The Egyptian Christians who are persecuted and imprisoned for worshipping Jesus.

Ethiopia - Eastern Africa

Population: 52,569,000
Capital: Addis Ababa
Language: Amharic, Orominga, Tigrinya, Arabic
Christian: 58% (Evangelicals: 13%)
Muslim: 35%
Secular: 6%
Pray for:
- Rest and healing from famine, war and disease.
- Churches to be rebuilt and for Ethiopians to find hope in Jesus.

Fiji - Pacific

Population: 794,000
Capital: Suva
Language: English, Fijian, Hindi
Christian: 53.4% (Evangelicals: 10.4%)
Muslim 7.5%
Hindu: 37.3%
Pray for:
- More Christian workers among the Hindus and Muslims.
- Fijians to find hope and healing in Jesus from the pain of broken homes and alcohol abuse.

Greece - Southeastern Europe

Population: 10,124,000
Capital: Athens
Language: Greek
Christian: 98% (Evangelicals: 0.14%)
Muslim: 1.5%
Pray for:
- More freedom for Christians to share about their faith in Jesus in Greece.
- The many Greeks who have never really heard and understood the Gospel message.

India - Central Asia

Population: 904,800,000
Capital: New Delhi
Language: Hindi, English, other
Christian: 2.61% (Evangelicals: 1%)
Muslim: 12%
Buddhist: .7%
Hindu: 80.7%
Animist: 1.5%
Pray for:
- An end to the harsh treatment and conditions child laborers face each day.
- Christians to reach these children with God's love and the message of the Gospel.

Kenya - Eastern Africa

Population: 30,844,000
Capital: Nairobi
Language: English, KiSwahili, Kikuyu, other
Christian: 82.1% (Evangelicals: 34%)
Muslim: 6%
Animist: 10%
Pray for:

- More trained leaders and pastors to disciple the Kenyan Christians.
- Unity among believers based on the truth found in God's Word, not tribal customs.

Mexico - Central America

Population: 97,967,000
Capital: Mexico City
Language: Spanish, Indian Languages
Christian: 94.6% (Evangelicals: 4.3%)
Jewish: 0.1%
Secular: 5.3%

Pray for:
- The millions of poor people throughout Mexico and the many street children in Mexico City.
- Mexicans to use the Bible as a guide for their faith in God and in their daily lives.

Morocco - North Africa

Population: 29,116,000
Capital: Rabat
Language: Arabic, Berber, French
Christian: 0.15% (Evangelicals: 0.01%)
Jewish: 0.05%
Muslim: 99.8%

Pray for:
- Boldness and safety for the Christians in Morocco who are a witness for Jesus.
- Moroccans to seek and find salvation in Jesus Christ.

Russia - Eastern Europe

Population: 153,646,000
Capital: Moscow
Languages: Russian, other
Christian: 56.3% (Evangelicals: 0.56%)
Jewish: 0.4%
Muslim: 8.7%
Secular: 32.7%
Animist: 0.8%

Pray for:
- Continued freedom and greater stability as Russia continues its transition from Communism.
- More Bible schools to train the new generation of Christian leaders and pastors.
- More missionaries with a long-term calling to be equipped and sent to Russia.

United States - North America

Population: 258,204,000
Capital: Washington DC
Language: English
Christian: 86.5% (Evangelicals 30.3%)
Jewish: 2.4%
Muslim: 1.8%
Buddhist: 0.4%
Hindu: 0.2%

Pray for:
- True revival from God that crosses ethnic and denominational boundaries.
- American kids to find salvation and true meaning for their lives in Jesus Christ.

DEFINITIONS

Animism:
The belief that non-living objects (rocks, trees, sun, moon, etc.) and even the entire universe possess spirits or souls.

Atheism:
The belief that God does not exist.

Bazaar:
A marketplace where different kinds of goods are sold.

Buddhist:
A follower of the teachings of Gautama (called Buddha), who lived in India about 2,500 years ago. Many followers worship Gautama and spend time meditating, hoping to become pure enough to stop the believed cycle of death and rebirth called reincarnation.

Cocaine:
A dangerous and addictive drug processed from coca leaves and similar in appearance to white flour.

Communist:
A follower of the social/political system of Communism. This system typically consists of a single party government where private ownership of property is not allowed. Control in most areas of society is by the central government.

Evangelicals:
Christian believers who recognize the authority of the Bible as the guide for their faith and actions. A central doctrine among Evangelicals is the necessity of a relationship with, and personal faith in Jesus Christ for salvation.

Hindu:
A follower of the religion that teaches the existence of thousands of different gods. A major Hindu belief is reincarnation. This belief teaches that after dying, people come back to life again as animals or people. Hindus believe that how they behave in their past life affects their place (caste) in this life, and their actions in this life will decide their place (caste) in their next life.

Islam:
The religious belief that Muhammad is the prophet of the one true God. Followers of Islam are called Muslims. Followers of Islam number over two hundred million worldwide.

Muslim: (see Islam)
Those people who practice the religion of Islam.
New Age:
A wide range of non-Christian beliefs and practices often composed of occultic or supernatural elements.
Non-religious/secular:
People who are not concerned with or a follower of any religion.
Orthodox:
A form of Christianity practiced in ancient times that is still in use in places today.
Poverty:
Very poor living conditions. People living in poverty have little or no food, money, or clothing.
Revival:
A widespread spiritual awakening among believers in a region or nation.
Rituals:
Formal or sacred acts used in religious ceremonies.

BIBLE READING PLAN: TRACK ONE

❏ Matthew 1, 2	❏ Luke 4	❏ Acts 7	❏ II Corinthians 1
❏ Matthew 3	❏ Luke 5	❏ Acts 8	❏ II Corinthians 2, 3
❏ Matthew 4	❏ Luke 6	❏ Acts 9	❏ II Corinthians 4, 5
❏ Matthew 5	❏ Luke 7	❏ Acts 10	❏ II Corinthians 6, 7
❏ Matthew 6, 7	❏ Luke 8	❏ Acts 11, 12	❏ II Corinthians 8
❏ Matthew 8	❏ Luke 9	❏ Acts 13	❏ II Corinthians 9, 10
❏ Matthew 9	❏ Luke 10	❏ Acts 14	❏ II Corinthians 11
❏ Matthew 10	❏ Luke 11	❏ Acts 15	❏ II Corinthians 12
❏ Matthew 11	❏ Luke 12	❏ Acts 16	❏ II Corinthians 13
❏ Matthew 12	❏ Luke 13	❏ Acts 17	❏ Galatians 1
❏ Matthew 13	❏ Luke 14	❏ Acts 18	❏ Galatians 2
❏ Matthew 14	❏ Luke 15	❏ Acts 19, 20	❏ Galatians 3
❏ Matthew 15	❏ Luke 16	❏ Acts 21	❏ Galatians 4
❏ Matthew 16	❏ Luke 17	❏ Acts 22	❏ Galatians 5
❏ Matthew 17	❏ Luke 18	❏ Acts 23	❏ Galatians 6
❏ Matthew 18	❏ Luke 19	❏ Acts 24, 25	❏ Ephesians 1
❏ Matthew 19	❏ Luke 20	❏ Acts 26	❏ Ephesians 2, 3
❏ Matthew 20	❏ Luke 21	❏ Acts 27, 28	❏ Ephesians 4
❏ Matthew 21	❏ Luke 22	❏ Romans 1	❏ Ephesians 5
❏ Matthew 22	❏ Luke 23	❏ Romans 2	❏ Ephesians 6
❏ Matthew 23	❏ Luke 24	❏ Romans 3	❏ Philippians 1
❏ Matthew 24	❏ John 1	❏ Romans 4	❏ Philippians 2
❏ Matthew 25	❏ John 2,3	❏ Romans 5	❏ Philippians 3, 4
❏ Matthew 26	❏ John 4	❏ Romans 6	❏ Colossians 1
❏ Matthew 27	❏ John 5	❏ Romans 7	❏ Colossians 2, 3
❏ Matthew 28	❏ John 6	❏ Romans 8	❏ Colossians 4
❏ Mark 1	❏ John 7	❏ Romans 9	❏ I Thessalonians 1, 2
❏ Mark 2	❏ John 8	❏ Romans 10	❏ I Thessalonians 3, 4
❏ Mark 3	❏ John 9	❏ Romans 11	❏ I Thessalonians 5
❏ Mark 4	❏ John 10	❏ Romans 12	❏ II Thessalonians 1, 2
❏ Mark 5	❏ John 11	❏ Romans 13	❏ II Thessalonians 3
❏ Mark 6	❏ John 12	❏ Romans 14	❏ I Timothy 1, 2
❏ Mark 7	❏ John 13	❏ Romans 15, 16	❏ I Timothy 3, 4
❏ Mark 8	❏ John 14	❏ I Corinthians 1	❏ I Timothy 5, 6
❏ Mark 9	❏ John 15	❏ I Corinthians 2, 3	❏ II Timothy 1, 2
❏ Mark 10	❏ John 16	❏ I Corinthians 4, 5	❏ II Timothy 3, 4
❏ Mark 11	❏ John 17	❏ I Corinthians 6	❏ Titus 1
❏ Mark 12	❏ John 18	❏ I Corinthians 7	❏ Titus 2, 3
❏ Mark 13	❏ John 19	❏ I Corinthians 8, 9	❏ Philemon
❏ Mark 14	❏ John 20, 21	❏ I Corinthians 10	❏ Hebrews 1
❏ Mark 15	❏ Acts 1	❏ I Corinthians 11	❏ Hebrews 2
❏ Mark 16	❏ Acts 2	❏ I Corinthians 12, 13	❏ Hebrews 3, 4
❏ Luke 1	❏ Acts 3	❏ I Corinthians 14	❏ Hebrews 5
❏ Luke 2	❏ Acts 4, 5	❏ I Corinthians 15	❏ Hebrews 6
❏ Luke 3	❏ Acts 6	❏ I Corinthians 16	❏ Hebrews 7, 8

- ❏ Hebrews 9
- ❏ Hebrews 10
- ❏ Hebrews 11
- ❏ Hebrews 12
- ❏ Hebrews 13
- ❏ James 1
- ❏ James 2
- ❏ James 3, 4
- ❏ James 5
- ❏ I Peter 1
- ❏ I Peter 2
- ❏ I Peter 3
- ❏ I Peter 4, 5
- ❏ II Peter 1
- ❏ II Peter 2
- ❏ II Peter 3
- ❏ I John 1, 2
- ❏ I John 3, 4
- ❏ I John 5
- ❏ II John, III John
- ❏ Jude
- ❏ Revelation 1
- ❏ Revelation 2
- ❏ Revelation 3
- ❏ Revelation 4, 5
- ❏ Revelation 6, 7
- ❏ Revelation 8, 9
- ❏ Revelation 10, 11
- ❏ Revelation 12, 13
- ❏ Revelation 14, 15
- ❏ Revelation 16, 17
- ❏ Revelation 18
- ❏ Revelation 19
- ❏ Revelation 20
- ❏ Revelation 21
- ❏ Revelation 22
- ❏ Psalm 1
- ❏ Psalm 2
- ❏ Psalm 3
- ❏ Psalm 4
- ❏ Psalm 5
- ❏ Psalm 6
- ❏ Psalm 7
- ❏ Psalm 8
- ❏ Psalm 9
- ❏ Psalm 10
- ❏ Psalm 11

- ❏ Psalm 12
- ❏ Psalm 13
- ❏ Psalm 14
- ❏ Psalm 15
- ❏ Psalm 16
- ❏ Psalm 17
- ❏ Psalm 18
- ❏ Psalm 19
- ❏ Psalm 20
- ❏ Psalm 21
- ❏ Psalm 22
- ❏ Psalm 23
- ❏ Psalm 24
- ❏ Psalm 25
- ❏ Psalm 26
- ❏ Psalm 27
- ❏ Psalm 28
- ❏ Psalm 29
- ❏ Psalm 30
- ❏ Psalm 31
- ❏ Psalm 32
- ❏ Psalm 33
- ❏ Psalm 34
- ❏ Psalm 35
- ❏ Psalm 36
- ❏ Psalm 37
- ❏ Psalm 38
- ❏ Psalm 39
- ❏ Psalm 40
- ❏ Psalm 41
- ❏ Psalm 42
- ❏ Psalm 43
- ❏ Psalm 44
- ❏ Psalm 45
- ❏ Psalm 46
- ❏ Psalm 47
- ❏ Psalm 48
- ❏ Psalm 49
- ❏ Psalm 50
- ❏ Psalm 51
- ❏ Psalm 52
- ❏ Psalm 53
- ❏ Psalm 54
- ❏ Psalm 55
- ❏ Psalm 56
- ❏ Psalm 57
- ❏ Psalm 58

- ❏ Psalm 59
- ❏ Psalm 60
- ❏ Psalm 61
- ❏ Psalm 62
- ❏ Psalm 63
- ❏ Psalm 64
- ❏ Psalm 65
- ❏ Psalm 66
- ❏ Psalm 67
- ❏ Psalm 68
- ❏ Psalm 69
- ❏ Psalm 70
- ❏ Psalm 71
- ❏ Psalm 72
- ❏ Psalm 73
- ❏ Psalm 74
- ❏ Psalm 75
- ❏ Psalm 76
- ❏ Psalm 77
- ❏ Psalm 78
- ❏ Psalm 79
- ❏ Psalm 80
- ❏ Psalm 81
- ❏ Psalm 82
- ❏ Psalm 83
- ❏ Psalm 84
- ❏ Psalm 85
- ❏ Psalm 86
- ❏ Psalm 87
- ❏ Psalm 88
- ❏ Psalm 89
- ❏ Psalm 90
- ❏ Psalm 91
- ❏ Psalm 92
- ❏ Psalm 93
- ❏ Psalm 94
- ❏ Psalm 95
- ❏ Psalm 96
- ❏ Psalm 97
- ❏ Psalm 98
- ❏ Psalm 99
- ❏ Psalm 100
- ❏ Psalm 101
- ❏ Psalm 102
- ❏ Psalm 103
- ❏ Psalm 104
- ❏ Psalm 105

- ❏ Psalm 106
- ❏ Psalm 107
- ❏ Psalm 108
- ❏ Psalm 109
- ❏ Psalm 110
- ❏ Psalm 111
- ❏ Psalm 112
- ❏ Psalm 113
- ❏ Psalm 114
- ❏ Psalm 115
- ❏ Psalm 116
- ❏ Psalm 117
- ❏ Psalm 118
- ❏ Psalm 119: 1-88
- ❏ Psalm 119: 89-176
- ❏ Psalm 120
- ❏ Psalm 121
- ❏ Psalm 122
- ❏ Psalm 123, 124
- ❏ Psalm 125
- ❏ Psalm 126
- ❏ Psalm 127, 128
- ❏ Psalm 129
- ❏ Psalm 130
- ❏ Psalm 131
- ❏ Psalm 132
- ❏ Psalm 133
- ❏ Psalm 134
- ❏ Psalm 135
- ❏ Psalm 136
- ❏ Psalm 137
- ❏ Psalm 138
- ❏ Psalm 139
- ❏ Psalm 140
- ❏ Psalm 141
- ❏ Psalm 142
- ❏ Psalm 143
- ❏ Psalm 144
- ❏ Psalm 145
- ❏ Psalm 146
- ❏ Psalm 147
- ❏ Psalm 148
- ❏ Psalm 149
- ❏ Psalm 150

BIBLE READING PLAN: TRACK TWO

- ❏ Genesis 1-3
- ❏ Genesis 4-6
- ❏ Genesis 7-9
- ❏ Genesis 10-12
- ❏ Genesis 13-15
- ❏ Genesis 16-18
- ❏ Genesis 19-21
- ❏ Genesis 22-24
- ❏ Genesis 25-27
- ❏ Genesis 28-30
- ❏ Genesis 31-33
- ❏ Genesis 34-36
- ❏ Genesis 37-39
- ❏ Genesis 40-42
- ❏ Genesis 43-45
- ❏ Genesis 46-48
- ❏ Genesis 49-50
- ❏ Exodus 1-3
- ❏ Exodus 4-6
- ❏ Exodus 7-9
- ❏ Exodus 10-12
- ❏ Exodus 13-15
- ❏ Exodus 16-18
- ❏ Exodus 19-21
- ❏ Exodus 22-24
- ❏ Exodus 25-27
- ❏ Exodus 28-30
- ❏ Exodus 31-33
- ❏ Exodus 34-36
- ❏ Exodus 37-40
- ❏ Leviticus 1, 2
- ❏ Leviticus 3, 4
- ❏ Leviticus 5, 6
- ❏ Leviticus 7, 8
- ❏ Leviticus 9
- ❏ Leviticus 10, 11
- ❏ Leviticus 12, 13
- ❏ Leviticus 14, 15
- ❏ Leviticus 16, 17
- ❏ Leviticus 18, 19
- ❏ Leviticus 20, 21
- ❏ Leviticus 22, 23
- ❏ Leviticus 24, 25
- ❏ Leviticus 26, 27
- ❏ Numbers 1-3

- ❏ Numbers 4-6
- ❏ Numbers 7-9
- ❏ Numbers 10-12
- ❏ Numbers 13-15
- ❏ Numbers 16-18
- ❏ Numbers 19-21
- ❏ Numbers 22-24
- ❏ Numbers 25-27
- ❏ Numbers 28-30
- ❏ Numbers 31-33
- ❏ Numbers 34-36
- ❏ Deuteronomy 1-3
- ❏ Deuteronomy 4-6
- ❏ Deuteronomy 7-9
- ❏ Deuteronomy 10-12
- ❏ Deuteronomy 13-15
- ❏ Deuteronomy 16-18
- ❏ Deuteronomy 19-21
- ❏ Deuteronomy 22-24
- ❏ Deuteronomy 25-27
- ❏ Deuteronomy 28-30
- ❏ Deuteronomy 31-34
- ❏ Joshua 1-4
- ❏ Joshua 5-8
- ❏ Joshua 9-12
- ❏ Joshua 13-16
- ❏ Joshua 17-20
- ❏ Joshua 21-24
- ❏ Judges 1-3
- ❏ Judges 4-6
- ❏ Judges 7-9
- ❏ Judges 10-12
- ❏ Judges 13-15
- ❏ Judges 16-18
- ❏ Judges 19-21
- ❏ Ruth 1-4
- ❏ I Samuel 1-3
- ❏ I Samuel 4-6
- ❏ I Samuel 7-9
- ❏ I Samuel 10-12
- ❏ I Samuel 13-15
- ❏ I Samuel 16-18
- ❏ I Samuel 19-21
- ❏ I Samuel 22-24
- ❏ I Samuel 25-27

- ❏ I Samuel 28, 29
- ❏ I Samuel 30, 31
- ❏ II Samuel 1-3
- ❏ II Samuel 4-6
- ❏ II Samuel 7-9
- ❏ II Samuel 10-12
- ❏ II Samuel 13-15
- ❏ II Samuel 16-18
- ❏ II Samuel 19-21
- ❏ II Samuel 22-24
- ❏ I Kings 1-3
- ❏ I Kings 4-6
- ❏ I Kings 7-9
- ❏ I Kings 10-12
- ❏ I Kings 13-15
- ❏ I Kings 16-18
- ❏ I Kings 19-22
- ❏ II Kings 1-3
- ❏ II Kings 4-6
- ❏ II Kings 7-9
- ❏ II Kings 10-12
- ❏ II Kings 13-15
- ❏ II Kings 16-18
- ❏ II Kings 19-21
- ❏ II Kings 22-25
- ❏ I Chronicles 1-3
- ❏ I Chronicles 4-6
- ❏ I Chronicles 7-9
- ❏ I Chronicles 10-12
- ❏ I Chronicles 13-15
- ❏ I Chronicles 16-18
- ❏ I Chronicles 19-21
- ❏ I Chronicles 22-24
- ❏ I Chronicles 25-27
- ❏ I Chronicles 28, 29
- ❏ II Chronicles 1-3
- ❏ II Chronicles 4-6
- ❏ II Chronicles 7-9
- ❏ II Chronicles 10-12
- ❏ II Chronicles 13-15
- ❏ II Chronicles 16-18
- ❏ II Chronicles 19-21
- ❏ II Chronicles 22-24
- ❏ II Chronicles 25-27
- ❏ II Chronicles 28-30

- ❏ II Chronicles 31-33
- ❏ II Chronicles 34-36
- ❏ Ezra 1-3
- ❏ Ezra 4-6
- ❏ Ezra 7-10
- ❏ Nehemiah 1-3
- ❏ Nehemiah 4-6
- ❏ Nehemiah 7-9
- ❏ Nehemiah 10-13
- ❏ Esther 1-3
- ❏ Esther 4-6
- ❏ Esther 7-10
- ❏ Job 1-3
- ❏ Job 4-6
- ❏ Job 7-9
- ❏ Job 10-12
- ❏ Job 13-15
- ❏ Job 16-18
- ❏ Job 19-21
- ❏ Job 22-24
- ❏ Job 25-27
- ❏ Job 28-30
- ❏ Job 31-33
- ❏ Job 34-36
- ❏ Job 37-39
- ❏ Job 40-42
- ❏ Psalm 1-3
- ❏ Psalm 4-6
- ❏ Psalm 7-9
- ❏ Psalm 10-12
- ❏ Psalm 13-15
- ❏ Psalm 16-18
- ❏ Psalm 19-21
- ❏ Psalm 22-24
- ❏ Psalm 25-27
- ❏ Psalm 28-30
- ❏ Psalm 31-33
- ❏ Psalm 34-36
- ❏ Tsalm 37-39
- ❏ Psalm 40-42
- ❏ Psalm 43-45
- ❏ Psalm 46-48
- ❏ Psalm 49-51
- ❏ Psalm 52-54
- ❏ Psalm 55-57

- ❏ Psalm 58-60
- ❏ Psalm 61-63
- ❏ Psalm 64-66
- ❏ Psalm 67-69
- ❏ Psalm 70-72
- ❏ Psalm 73-75
- ❏ Psalm 76-78
- ❏ Psalm 79-81
- ❏ Psalm 82-84
- ❏ Psalm 85-87
- ❏ Psalm 88-90
- ❏ Psalm 91-93
- ❏ Psalm 94-96
- ❏ Psalm 97-100
- ❏ Psalm 101-103
- ❏ Psalm 104-106
- ❏ Psalm 107-109
- ❏ Psalm 110-113
- ❏ Psalm 114-118
- ❏ Psalm 119
- ❏ Psalm 120-123
- ❏ Psalm 124-128
- ❏ Psalm 129-133
- ❏ Psalm 134-138
- ❏ Psalm 139-141
- ❏ Psalm 142-145
- ❏ Psalm 146-150
- ❏ Proverbs 1-3
- ❏ Proverbs 4-6
- ❏ Proverbs 7-9
- ❏ Proverbs 10-12
- ❏ Proverbs 13-15
- ❏ Proverbs 16-18
- ❏ Proverbs 19-21
- ❏ Proverbs 22-24
- ❏ Proverbs 25-27
- ❏ Proverbs 28-31
- ❏ Ecclesiastes 1-4
- ❏ Ecclesiastes 5-8
- ❏ Ecclesiastes 9-12
- ❏ Song of Songs 1-4
- ❏ Song of Songs 5-8
- ❏ Isaiah 1-3
- ❏ Isaiah 4-6
- ❏ Isaiah 7-9
- ❏ Isaiah 10-12
- ❏ Isaiah 13-15
- ❏ Isaiah 16-18
- ❏ Isaiah 19-21
- ❏ Isaiah 22-24
- ❏ Isaiah 25-27
- ❏ Isaiah 28-30
- ❏ Isaiah 31-33
- ❏ Isaiah 34-36
- ❏ Isaiah 37-39
- ❏ Isaiah 40-42
- ❏ Isaiah 43-45
- ❏ Isaiah 46-48
- ❏ Isaiah 49-51
- ❏ Isaiah 52-54
- ❏ Isaiah 55-57
- ❏ Isaiah 58-60
- ❏ Isaiah 61-63
- ❏ Isaiah 63-66
- ❏ Jeremiah 1-3
- ❏ Jeremiah 4-6
- ❏ Jeremiah 7-9
- ❏ Jeremiah 10-12
- ❏ Jeremiah 13-15
- ❏ Jeremiah 16-18
- ❏ Jeremiah 19-21
- ❏ Jeremiah 22-24
- ❏ Jeremiah 25-27
- ❏ Jeremiah 28-30
- ❏ Jeremiah 31-33
- ❏ Jeremiah 34-36
- ❏ Jeremiah 37-39
- ❏ Jeremiah 40-42
- ❏ Jeremiah 43-45
- ❏ Jeremiah 46-48
- ❏ Jeremiah 49-52
- ❏ Lamentations 1-5
- ❏ Ezekiel 1-3
- ❏ Ezekiel 4-6
- ❏ Ezekiel 7-9
- ❏ Ezekiel 10-12
- ❏ Ezekiel 13-15
- ❏ Ezekiel 16-18
- ❏ Ezekiel 19-21
- ❏ Ezekiel 22-24
- ❏ Ezekiel 25-27
- ❏ Ezekiel 28-30
- ❏ Ezekiel 31-33
- ❏ Ezekiel 34-36
- ❏ Ezekiel 37-39
- ❏ Ezekiel 40-42
- ❏ Ezekiel 43-45
- ❏ Ezekiel 46-48
- ❏ Daniel 1-4
- ❏ Daniel 5-8
- ❏ Daniel 9-12
- ❏ Hosea 1-3
- ❏ Hosea 4-7
- ❏ Hosea 8-10
- ❏ Hosea 11-14
- ❏ Joel 1-3
- ❏ Amos 1-3
- ❏ Amos 4-6
- ❏ Amos 7-9
- ❏ Obadiah, Jonah 1-4
- ❏ Micah 1-3
- ❏ Micah 4-7
- ❏ Nahum 1-3
- ❏ Habakkuk 1-3
- ❏ Zephaniah 1-3
- ❏ Haggai 1-2
- ❏ Zechariah 1-4
- ❏ Zechariah 5-9
- ❏ Zechariah 10-14
- ❏ Malachi 1-4
- ❏ Matthew 1-5
- ❏ Matthew 6-10
- ❏ Matthew 11-15
- ❏ Matthew 16-20
- ❏ Matthew 21-25
- ❏ Matthew 26-28
- ❏ Mark 1-5
- ❏ Mark 6-10
- ❏ Mark 11-16
- ❏ Luke 1-5
- ❏ Luke 6-10
- ❏ Luke 11-15
- ❏ Luke 16-20
- ❏ Luke 21-24
- ❏ John 1-4
- ❏ John 5-8
- ❏ John 9-12
- ❏ John 13-16
- ❏ John 17-21
- ❏ Acts 1-3
- ❏ Acts 4-6
- ❏ Acts 7-9
- ❏ Acts 10-12
- ❏ Acts 13-15
- ❏ Acts 16-18
- ❏ Acts 19-22
- ❏ Acts 23-28
- ❏ Romans 1-3
- ❏ Romans 4-6
- ❏ Romans 7-9
- ❏ Romans 10-12
- ❏ Romans 13-16
- ❏ I Corinthians 1-3
- ❏ I Corinthians 4-6
- ❏ I Corinthians 7-9
- ❏ I Corinthians 10-12
- ❏ I Corinthians 13-16
- ❏ II Corinthians 1-4
- ❏ II Corinthians 5-8
- ❏ II Corinthians 9-13
- ❏ Galatians 1-3
- ❏ Galatians 4-6
- ❏ Ephesians 1-3
- ❏ Ephesians 4-6
- ❏ Philippians 1-4
- ❏ Colossians 1-4
- ❏ I Thessalonians 1-5
- ❏ II Thessalonians 1-3
- ❏ I Timothy 1-6
- ❏ II Timothy 1-4
- ❏ Titus 1-3, Philemon
- ❏ Hebrews 1-3
- ❏ Hebrews 4-6
- ❏ Hebrews 7-9
- ❏ Hebrews 10-13
- ❏ James 1-5
- ❏ I Peter 1-5
- ❏ II Peter 1-3
- ❏ I John 1-5
- ❏ II John, III John, Jude
- ❏ Revelation 1-4
- ❏ Revelation 5-8
- ❏ Revelation 9-12
- ❏ Revelation 13-15
- ❏ Revelation 16-18
- ❏ Revelation 19-22

TrAcKiNG YoUr...

FAMILY & FRIENDS

NAME:

ADDRESS:

CITY:

TELEPHONE:

NAME:

ADDRESS:

CITY:

TELEPHONE:

NAME:

ADDRESS:

CITY:

TELEPHONE:

NAME:

ADDRESS:

CITY:

TELEPHONE:

NAME:

ADDRESS:

CITY:

TELEPHONE:

TrAcKiNG YoUr...

FAMILY & FRIENDS

NAME:

ADDRESS:

CITY:

TELEPHONE:

NAME:

ADDRESS:

CITY:

TELEPHONE:

NAME:

ADDRESS:

CITY:

TELEPHONE:

NAME:

ADDRESS:

CITY:

TELEPHONE:

NAME:

ADDRESS:

CITY:

TELEPHONE:

TrAcKiNG YoUr...

FAMILY & FRIENDS

NAME:

ADDRESS:

CITY:

TELEPHONE:

NAME:

ADDRESS:

CITY:

TELEPHONE:

NAME:

ADDRESS:

CITY:

TELEPHONE:

NAME:

ADDRESS:

CITY:

TELEPHONE:

NAME:

ADDRESS:

CITY:

TELEPHONE:

TrAcKiNG YoUr...

NOTES

TrAcKiNG YoUr...

NOTES

TrAcKiNG YoUr...

NOTES

NOTES

TrAcKiNG YoUr...

NOTES

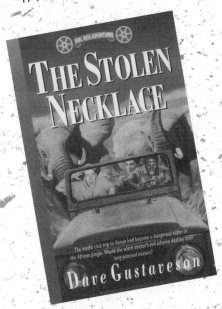
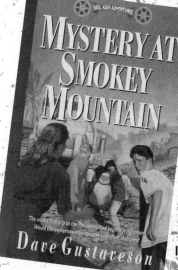

Resources To Help You Get Involved in

WORLD EVANGELISM:

• KING'S KIDS

King's Kids is a ministry of Youth With A Mission in partnership with families and the local church. King's Kids provides opportunities for youth to be involved in outreach programs at local, national and international levels using the performing arts, service skills and sports.

IN U.S. OR CANADA, CONTACT:

King's Kids Canada
Box 3303
Vancouver, BC V6B 3Y3
Canada
Phone: 1-604-850-5437

OUTSIDE THE U.S. OR CANADA, CONTACT:

King's Kids International
P.O. Box 117
Kailua-Kona, HI 96745-0117
U.S.A.
Phone: 1-808-329-5745

• DANIEL PRAYER GROUPS

A ministry of King's Kids, designed to involve children, teens and families in the ministry of intercession for the world. For more information on how you can join in prayer with youth from all over the world...

CONTACT:

King's Kids /Daniel Prayer Groups
Stanely House 14, Stanely Crescent
Paisley PA2 9LF
Scotland, United Kingdom

• ESTHER NETWORK INTERNATIONAL

The Esther Network is mobilizing children and young people to pray for their generation and the issues that concern them. They offer helpful "PRAYERTOOLS" such as the "GLOBALL" (a soft, colorful globe of the world), Prayer Spinner, Impression Ball, 10/40 Window "How-to" Manual, song/music cassette, etc. to focus prayer on the children/youth of the nations. For more information and a catalog, contact:

ESTHER NETWORK INTERNATIONAL

854 Conniston Road
West Palm Beach, FL 33405-2131
U.S.A.
Phone: 1-407-832-6490
Fax: 1-407-832-8043